Dedicated to the staff and congregation of First United Methodist Church in Downtown Bentonville, Arkansas, who go along with all my crazy ideas. Including dressing up as different generations and coming to worship in costume like some sort of holy Spirit Week. Or Holy Spirit Week, if you prefer.

A special thanks to those who helped preach this series as representatives of their generations: Rev. Dr. Don Hall (Silent), Rev. Dr. Ray Wheeler (Boomer), Kristin Wells (Millennial), and Brooke Tilley (Gen Z). Also thanks to an amazing staff willing to make these wild ideas come to life that includes Ken Weatherford, Matt Nelson, Lexie Burleson, Allison Earhart, Jonathan Day, Chandra Rogers, Matt Bridges, and Johnna Kosnoff.

PROPHETS
TO THE GENERATIONS

HOW GOD RAISES PROPHETS FROM
ISAIAH TO GEN Z AND BEYOND

Jeremiäs Martin Malala Daniel

MICHELLE J. MORRIS

Prophets to the Generations

How God Raises Prophets from ISAIAH to Gen Z and Beyond

©2026 Michelle J. Morris
books@marketsquarebooks.com
141 N. Martinwood, Suite 2 Knoxville, Tennessee 37923

ISBN: 978-1-950899-98-2

Printed and Bound in the United States of America
Cover Illustration & Book Design ©2025 Market Square Publishing, LLC

Editor: Sheri Carder Hood
Cover Design: Kevin Slimp
Page Design: Ashley Burton

Scripture quotations used with permission from:

NRSVUE

CEB

Contents

When I asked a friend of mine to come

up with some characteristics of prophets,

he responded, "Prophets are weird."

He's not wrong.

CHAPTER ONE
Prophets To...

I hesitate to start this chapter with a title that includes an ellipsis (...) because, according to the debates about generations on TikTok, everyone knows that if there is an ellipsis, a Gen Xer is behind it. For this book, however, it is best that I just own who I am so you know where I stand in our current generational realities.

Debates about the traits of generations seem to occupy a great deal of social media, news reports, blogs, and books these days. I am sitting here composing such a work, so I'd better not throw stones from the glass house I sit in. Truly, I am fascinated by the broad distinctions among the generations. As the lead pastor of a large United Methodist Church in Arkansas, I have the privilege of actually serving all eight living generations.[1] As their pastor, I must understand their diverse perspectives and experiences, even as I acknowledge that the individuals who come to me will not perfectly fit the characteristics of their generation.

---

[1] The generations are as follows: Greatest (born before 1925); Silent (b. 1925-1944); Boomers (b. 1945-1964); Gen X (b. 1965-1980); Millennials (b. 1981-1996); Gen Z (b. 1997-2012); Gen Alpha (b.2013-2024); Gen Beta (b. 2025+). Actual year breakdowns are subject to debate. People born in the years that mark the changes to a new generation usually have characteristics of both.

Where we are all gathered together, however, is in worship and church-wide events that are truly intergenerational, like the good old church potluck. To promote unity amidst all the diversity, not only do I need to understand the myriad perspectives of my people, but I also need them to understand each other.

In addition to the work of helping people understand each other's stories, it is also my role as their spiritual leader to help them understand God's story as contained in the Old and New Testaments. I find that most regular churchgoers are fairly familiar with the Gospels (even if we don't always successfully put what we know into practice). They probably also know something about Genesis and the high points of Exodus. My population is also aware of Revelation, but they don't tend to study it, largely out of fear for what they think it contains or because wrestling with all the symbolism seems like a monumental task. They know Psalms because they have sung them (Ecclesiastes, too, if they are Boomers who know The Byrds), and Proverbs because they have quoted them. They know Paul existed and wrote letters, and they know Job had a rough few weeks. But the history books, the scrolls, and many of the letters are not familiar to them in any depth, typically.

And then there are the prophets.

Few of us have more than just a passing awareness of the prophets, except for Isaiah, whose words are quoted in

Advent, Micah 6:8, and Jeremiah 29:11, which make their way onto embroidered pillows. Some believe the prophets are not worth engaging with because they speak into a very particular time and situation, something that has long since passed. There is some truth to that, of course. But then the same could be argued of Paul's letters, and really of most of the Bible. Even some of Jesus' lessons use images that are largely unfamiliar in our modern world. How many of us encounter sheep and shepherds on the regular these days?

There are particularities in all the books of the Bible, but there are universal joys and struggles and timeless words of wisdom throughout them all as well. Another wonderful thing about the Bible is that you can read a passage one day, and it will have one meaning for you; then, a few years later, you read that same passage, and it means something totally different. But it still has meaning. It is just shaped differently depending on where you stand in your life history.

Out of the twin needs to help my then seven generations understand each other and the prophets better, we spent the summer of 2023 in a sermon series that shares the name of the book: *Prophets to the Generations.* I noticed that you can pair each one of the major generations (sorry, Greatest Generation and Gen Alpha) with one of the major prophets. The series helped my people not only see the different perspectives around them, but it also gave them a means to hold on to the distinct characteristics of the major prophets. It also showed us in concrete terms that the Bible is still very much a living text, still speaking into our new realities. We still need God's word, we still need to understand our story in light of God's story, and we still need God's prophets to help us in that understanding.

What is a Prophet?

Before we get too deep in the weeds of the characteristics of the prophets, let's step back and understand some basics on the work of a prophet, starting with the definition of what a "prophet" is. More than once, I have asked people to give me a definition of a "prophet." My favorite answer to that question came from a fifth grader in Vacation Bible School. Her hand shot up with wild enthusiasm, so I asked her to share with all of us what a prophet is. She said, "It's the amount of money a business makes that they get to keep!"

"You are absolutely right," I said. "You have perfectly described a profit. That 'profit' is spelled p-r-o-f-i-t. Now, can anyone tell me what a prophet is if I spell it p-r-o-p-h-e-t?"

Crickets.

It is not surprising that fifth graders don't understand prophets. Many adults don't either. The most typical answer I get when asking adults to define "prophet" is "Someone who tells the future." That answer is partially right, but it also creates some significant confusion. Prophets are not fortune tellers. Prophets are *truth tellers*.

What is the difference? Fortune tellers, like prophets, are keen observers of the world around them. They deliberately call on magical elements to support their claims. Their revelations are also usually reserved for individuals. Prophets not only have keen observational skills, but they are also masters of common sense. They look at situations with a critical eye, and in so doing, they can foresee the consequences of actions. It is a bit like when you are a parent raising a child who has to push every boundary and prove everything for themselves. You know that no matter how many times you tell that child they shouldn't touch a hot stove, the day will come when they touch the stove anyway, because they have to satisfy their own curiosity, and they don't just do as they are told.

Prophets foresee the consequences of the path the people have chosen to travel, and they try to get their attention to head off the damage. They also know that the likelihood of people listening to them is slim, but they have to try anyway. Occasionally, a prophet's message will be directed at an individual, but that individual is exclusively someone with significant power, like when Nathan called out David. The prophet knows that the individual influences the whole people, so really, that work is as communally directed as their oracles to the nations are.

So the foresight that prophets have does not come from magic potions or crystal balls. It comes from understanding that actions have consequences. We see that play out in the conversations between God and God's prophets. God shares what is going to happen, the prophet understands those consequences, and may even try to argue for another chance for the people. In fact, the prophet is often the last-ditch chance the people have. All the prophet has to do is get them to listen. But how exactly are they going to do that?

How Do Prophets Get Our Attention?

When I asked a friend of mine to come up with some characteristics of prophets, he responded, "Prophets are weird." He's not wrong. Perhaps because they are not aligned with the way things are going, they naturally stand apart from the people. But they also deeply love the people, even if they are mad at them most of the time.

Another reason they are weird is because part of their work involves prophetic actions. These are actions that prophets take that are so bizarre, they get noticed. They are also distinctly linked to the message they are trying to convey to the people. Take, for instance, Ezekiel, who is told to lie on his left side for 390 days, with one day representing one year of Israel's sin against God. Then he has to lie on his right side for forty days to represent the number of years of sin from Judah—that is, after building a diorama of the siege of Jerusalem at the same time as he had to eat bread cooked over dung to represent the coming famine.

Those kinds of actions get people talking. As people are talking, hopefully, they are also discussing the purported meanings behind these actions. Ideally, they would also change their ways, but in the case of the biblical prophets, only one—Jonah— actually succeeds in getting people to change. And in Jonah, the people change almost despite him.

But the actions do remain in the memory of the people. As they then watch the warnings become reality, the people understand the chance they had. They preserve those stories, and hopefully, those stories either delay or prevent future problems. As part of the biblical canon, they also give us concrete images to understand what God wants from us, as well as the consequences we face when we stray from God's will. No matter what happens, the prophet has done their job in laying bare reality before the people. And because we seem to constantly need reminders of the consequences of our actions, prophets continue to be needed to this day.

Who is a Prophet's Audience?

You have probably heard the adage, "Those who are ignorant of history are doomed to repeat it." As you read through the prophets, seeing the same issues coming up in every single book, it will start to sound monotonous. But it also proves the proverbial point: we keep repeating the same mistakes over and over and over again.

Of course, some of the monotony comes from the fact that most of the prophets in our canon were written just before the two exiles (Assyrian in 701 BCE and Babylonian in 587 BCE), during the exiles, or in the years after the return home (beginning around 539 BCE). Isaiah may actually cover the entire Assyrian/Babylonian period before, during, and after that stretch of time.

It might seem, then, that the audience to whom the

prophets speak also remains the same. In a broad sense, that is true, because our biblical prophets are specifically addressing the Israelite and Judean followers of God. But within that broad stroke are several variables. It matters whether a prophet is warning about a siege that is seventy years away versus warning about a siege because the Babylonian army has surrounded Jerusalem. It matters whether the prophet has the ear of the king or if the prophet is amongst the people. It matters whether the prophet is speaking to people who feel lost and hopeless because they are in exile or if the people are overcome with joy because they are finally being allowed to return home. It is in those distinctions that the differences in the biblical prophets are found.

Now, do we still need these prophets? Their context is long gone to us. What do the words for a people going into or coming out of exile have to do with us? Nothing. And everything. Have you ever left home and found yourself sort of spinning, trying to figure out who you are now? The entire world just experienced a mass exile in the shelter we took during the COVID-19 pandemic. Were there warnings we could have heeded ahead of that time to control the damage? Yes, there were. If we ignore the historically bound specifics of the biblical prophets and focus on their messages about caring for the vulnerable, controlling wealth, responsible consumption, fair treatment for the stranger, being careful about political entanglements, and listening to and following God, we can see that the message of the prophets is as alive for us now as it was then.

And then, because history does seem to be cyclical, we can actually find repetitions in history, again, if we aren't so specific as to look out our windows and expect to see the Babylonian army surrounding our town. That cyclical nature of history is what has given rise to this book. As we look at the five central generations alive today, we will find for each one a companion prophet, a prophet who shared in similar struggles and relished similar hopes. And hope will be present in all cases. For no matter how hard life gets in any given moment, we can trust that God is ultimately leading us all toward the good. We will also find that God has already sent us a prophet: one who will challenge us and call us to accountability and one who will also inspire us with hope.

One more note about the audiences. As we move through the generations, I will use broad strokes to characterize each one. I have already noted that no one person will fit 100 percent of their generation's characteristics. I also need to note that there is significant debate about what characteristics broadly fit a generation. There are many ways to approach such characterizations. For this work, I have relied primarily on two books to help frame the conversation: *Sticking Points: How to Get Five Generations Working Together in the Twelve Places They Come Apart* by Haydn Shaw,[2] and *Generations: The Real Difference Between Gen Z, Millennials, Gen X, Boomers, and Silents – And What*

---

[2] Haydn Shaw, *Sticking Points: How to Get Five Generations Working Together in the Twelve Places They Come Apart* (Carol Stream, IL: Tyndale House, 2013).

They Mean for America's Future by Jean M. Twenge, Ph.D.[3]

Twenge conducts extensive statistical analysis, while Shaw examines how the historical experiences of the generations, particularly during late childhood and early adulthood when worldviews tend to crystallize, shape the generations' understanding of the world and their place in it. In general, prophets do not have to confront statistics. They have to confront narratives. Prophets are trying to dislodge unhelpful worldviews, which they can only do with a more compelling story, and they are trying to replace rumors or heresies with God's truth. Shaw's goal is to bring the generations together through a greater understanding of our worldviews. Twenge is simply trying to provide a more accurate picture of the constitution of each generation with some attention to what that means for us, but cooperation is not the heart of her particular work. Since the ways we narrate our identities are a key factor in our worldviews, I will occasionally look at how generations are characterized in pop culture (TikTok, YouTube, etc.), because that tells us a great deal about the generations' self-definitions. Those narratives must be confronted, too.

Let the journey through the generations and our prophets begin.

---

[3] Jean M. Twenge, *Generations: The Real Difference Between Gen Z, Millennials, Gen X, Boomers, and Silents—and What They Mean for America's Future* (New York: Atria Books, 2023).

Discussion Questions:

1. What role does generational identity play in how people understand Scripture and their place in the church?

2. How can the actions and messages of the biblical prophets still resonate in today's culture of skepticism and disconnection?

3. What do you think distinguishes a prophet from a fortune teller in a modern context?

4. How does your church (or community) reflect the
   generational dynamics discussed in the chapter?

5. What prophetic voices—past or present—have helped shape
   your personal or spiritual journey?

Walter Cronkite

Technically a member of the Greatest Generation himself, he was a voice of calm for a chaotic world when he served as a news anchor in the 1960s and 1970s. In the midst of a growing Cold War and rising social turmoil, Cronkite was a steady voice at the mic. He echoed the trust in institutions and a calm belief in the overall good of humanity that the Silent Generation leaned on. Often referred to as "the most trusted man in America," Cronkite's take on the events of the day steadied a worried world, carrying people through World War II bombings, the Nuremberg trials, the Vietnam War, the assassinations of President John F. Kennedy and Martin Luther King Jr., Watergate, and the Iran Hostage Crisis. Through it all, he maintained clarity and composure. His own regular sign-off, "And that's the way it is," became a synonym for the Silent mantra, "Keep calm and carry on."

CHAPTER TWO
Isaiah and the Silent Generation
(b. 1925-1944)

Keep calm and carry on.

If there were ever a slogan to fit both Isaiah and the Silent Generation (Silents), that would be it. Life threw a great deal at the prophet and the people in their respective eras. And let's be honest—they both span an enormous stretch of time, especially considering the average human life span. Scholars believe that the material in Isaiah represents three distinct eras in the history of the Israelite/Judean people: the period preceding the Assyrian and Babylonian Exiles, the time of the exiles, and the early post-exilic period. This period spans a two-century time frame. As for the Silent Generation, they were born between 1925 and 1944, which means the eldest members of that generation have just reached centenarian status.

Both the prophets who spanned the centuries of exile and the Silents who spanned one hundred years in the 20th and 21st centuries have undergone significant shifts in their worldviews. Isaiah's original audience lived through the scattering of the first eleven tribes into the Diaspora, endured conquering by two brutal and powerful empires, and, with the fall of the Temple in Jerusalem, had to negotiate profound shifts in theology. They learned that God could continue to dwell with them outside the Temple and that they could remain God's people even when it felt like God had abandoned them to others. They also had to come to terms with the idea that God could work through Gentiles, as Cyrus, the king of Persia, created their path to return home.

As for the Silents, let's take just a moment to wonder at all they have seen. Both automobiles and planes were in their infancy when the first of the Silents came into the world. They were born in the unfolding of the Great Depression and the Second Great War. They came of age as the atomic bomb leveled Hiroshima and Nagasaki, and they were the young adults who had to find hope and peace in the face of conflicts around Communism and the Cold War. They have seen the creation of talking motion pictures, television, the internet, streaming services, and smartphones. They have watched newspapers and the *Yellow Pages* dominate communication and then fade into oblivion. They have seen men make it to the moon and watched two space shuttles blow up in midair. They have lived through World War II, Korea, Vietnam, the Gulf War, and September 11, 2001. They are the generation alive today who have seen it all—the good, the bad, and the ugly.

In the midst of so much change, the Silents have worked diligently to hold it together. They raised children (the Boomers) who were better off than they ever were. Despite such an overwhelming threat present in their lives since the dropping of the bomb, they have sought to build a stable, reliable foundation for society. While they may have a reputation for being the grumpy old people among us, they had a steady hand through some very difficult times. And they kept their hope alive—hope for our society, their children, grandchildren, and great-grandchildren.

The prophet Isaiah also held through difficult times and continued to proclaim hope amidst tremendous loss. Isaiah gives us the image of the suffering shepherd. Within Christianity, that image is often applied to Jesus. But it could also be applied to the people who navigated such tremendous shifts in worldview—the people of the exile and the Silent Generation today. Isaiah and the Silents reassure us of the persistence of humanity, and they reassure us that God will carry us through all things. "Keep calm and carry on," indeed.

Speaking Truth to Power

Now that we have set the stage for comparing Isaiah with the Silent Generation, let's drill down into more specifics. We will start with a key aspect of prophecy: speaking truth to power. Prophets know that the only way to enact change is through revolutionizing corrupt systems. You can go about such work in two ways: from the top down or from the bottom up. Both Isaiah and the Silents prefer to orchestrate such change from the top. Isaiah opens with a critique of those who are powerful, but by Chapter 7, we see Isaiah working with and encouraging King Hezekiah as he tries to navigate the political tensions around him. Isaiah's challenge is most often for the powerful, which, honestly, is the case for most prophecies. What is different about Isaiah is the relationship and trust that he has with the king. Normally, prophets are the bane of a king's existence; Isaiah is at times a trusted confidant. Isaiah seeks to right the path they are on, but he does so by working alongside power rather than against it.

Silents also seek to change things from within the system. This generation grew up watching the United States become a world power. They also saw us at a time when we took care of each other through devastation (Great Depression), took on immense evil (Hitler) and won, and harnessed the most powerful force in all creation (nuclear energy). As a result, this generation is very patriotic. It is not blind patriotism, though. It is a patriotism that sees the potential of what we can be: a moral, intellectual, and charitable force to be reckoned with. It's no wonder this generation seeks change from within existing systems.

What is an example of working within systems to enact change? Let's look at two landmark court cases: *Loving v. Virginia* and *Brown v. Board of Education of Topeka*. Both of these cases sought to dismantle aspects of racial discrimination in our legal code. The Lovings were arrested and jailed for being an interracial married couple. Linda Brown was a young African American girl who wanted to attend the less crowded white school located just a few blocks from her home. Both the Lovings and Linda Brown were successful in their fight, bringing a legal end to "separate but equal" and allowing people to marry without regard for color. What is important for this comparison, however, is that all of the plaintiffs were Silents. Linda Brown was born in 1942, and the Lovings were both born in the 1930s. They all worked within the court system to make prophetic change. They inherently acknowledged the value of our judicial system, even if it needed a push to come closer to the full inclusion of all its citizens.

The Power of the Sun

Perhaps the reason that Isaiah and Silents both work within the powers that be is simply because they deeply understand power. Power is never going away, nor will it be shared equally among people until we are in the fullness of God's reign. In light of this reality, the more power can be aimed toward good, the better. Both these groups have seen great power being used, and the possibility of that power being used for evil had to be guarded against at all costs. And what power had they seen? The power of the sun.

In Isaiah 38, Isaiah must deliver the news to King Hezekiah that he needs to get his affairs in order because he is going to die. Hezekiah wails and begs for healing. God instructs Isaiah to tell Hezekiah that he will, in fact, live fifteen more years. And, as a sign of that promise, God will move the sun backward ten steps after it has already shadowed all the steps of Ahaz. And God does exactly that. Such a miracle is not only a sign for the king that he will live longer, but it also shows the people where true power lies and what is possible when they follow God. By contrast, it should make anyone who doesn't follow God shake in their boots. This God can move the sun! Wouldn't it be in everyone's best interest to follow this God?

As for the Silents, I already mentioned that many of them came of age in the shadow of the atomic bomb. They were the first generation to reckon with nuclear power from childhood/early adulthood on. They carried the responsibility of guiding society through the nuclear age, which they did not technically start—the Greatest Generation gets that credit. As they watched world tensions rise and as two superpowers, the United States and the Soviet Union, vied for global dominance, they felt a strong duty not only toward their country but also to maintain peace. Like Isaiah, they saw the power of the sun manipulated in ways people may have imagined, but few really thought was possible. And like Isaiah, there was a recognition that such power could be used to change the course of history in either positive or negative ways. They fervently hoped for the former.

Population on the Move

As mentioned, the Book of Isaiah spans a time period from the beginning of the Assyrian conquest all the way through the return from the exiles. Exile brought with it significant changes in worldview. First, the people were scattered. Scattering brought them into daily contact with other cultures and religions and threatened to end their way of worshiping God. However, exile also invited them to see their God on a worldwide scale. This brought with it two innovations: worship in synagogues away from the Temple and a theology of inclusion in which Gentile God-fearers could see God as their own. It also facilitated the preservation of their story, which will be discussed later.

We see these innovations show up in various ways. First, there is the verse that is later applied to John the Baptist, with one small change in punctuation. In Matthew 3:3, the verse is translated, "A voice cries out in the wilderness, prepare the way of the Lord." However, Isaiah 40:3 reads, "A voice cries out, in the wilderness prepare the way of the Lord."[4] See the difference? The movement of the comma changes who is in the wilderness. In Matthew, it is John the Baptist. In Isaiah, it is the Lord who is in the wilderness. That's right. God wasn't confined to a destroyed Temple. God went with the people.

The opening of the faith to Gentiles probably also occurred as the Israelite/Judean people came into contact with others and shared about their faith. Their religion was also no longer confined to a small stretch of land. It was now spread wherever the people were spread, throughout the Assyrian and Babylonian empires. We see the prophetic hope for what that means in Isaiah Chapter 56, when immigrants and eunuchs[5] will be allowed to worship God, and God's "house will be known as a house of prayer for

---

[4] These are my own paraphrased translations designed to show the parallel, but they both do preserve the location of the comma in other translations.

[5] Eunuchs would have been barred from full worship at the Temple if the restriction to having mutilated genitals was maintained. This chapter lifts that restriction.

all peoples" (56:7). All nations would come to worship God. Strangely enough, it was the movement of the people that could make such a thing happen.

The Silents experienced a dramatic shift in their young lives as well: the move from farm to city. In his book *Sticking Points: How to Get Five Generations Working Together in the Twelve Places They Come Apart,* Haydn Shaw points out that in the early 20th century, two-thirds of Americans and Canadians lived on farms or in rural areas. By 1970, nearly 75 percent of the population lived in cities or suburbs.[6] That is an enormous migration that is rarely discussed when we examine shifts in morality and worldview. Shaw then goes on to identify four ways that migration shifted our culture:

- Life on the farm made it easier to instill a work ethic.
- Life on the farm provided meaningful adult roles at a young age.
- Life on the farm made it harder to commit crimes, abuse drugs, and become pregnant before marriage.
- Life on the farm is driven by the sun, not electricity.[7]

Think about those four points. Now think about where we are currently. We continue to wrestle with some of the problems that have arisen as a result of that migration. Others have simply shifted cultural perspectives. For instance, there is no longer significant condemnation of a woman and her child if that child was born outside of

---

[6] Haydn Shaw, *Sticking Points,* 63-64.

[7] Haydn Shaw, *Sticking Points,* 64-66.

marriage. In fact, many later generations have begun to eschew marriage altogether. Additionally, some of these changes have occurred as civil rights have been extended to more and more people. Some of that emancipation occurred when women poured into the workforce to help with production during World War II.

At least two of the generations discussed in this book (Millennials and Gen Z) have never really known a world with a significant rural reality. Boomers and Gen X participated in the movement. But Silents grew up in the rural world. That was foundational to who they are. The move to cities feels much more like an exile to that generation than to any of the others alive today. They have lived through the fullness of that migration, and they are still trying to navigate what that shift means to them. They also have had a burning question before them throughout their lives: how do we hold on to the values that still bring good to our lives?

Losing Everything, Saving What Matters

Both the people going into exile and the Silent Generation have experienced tremendous loss. Isaiah's audience experienced the destruction and violence of siege and scatter. Silents were children during the Great Depression and World War II. Such events of both timeframes have a way of implanting themselves in your psyche and never letting go. Along with such disruption comes a strong desire for preservation and conservation.

The important things about our societies must be saved.

It was during the twin exiles that the scholars and religious leaders of the Israelite and Judean people began compiling the Torah, which, in this context, refers to the first five books of the Hebrew Bible and our Old Testament. Genesis contains the origin stories. Exodus contains the defining story of Judaism, the account of the escape from slavery in Egypt. It also contains the basic organizing principles for the Jewish people to center around, defining them as God's chosen people. Leviticus continues the project of defining this people in the laws that shape how they are to relate to one another and to God. Numbers preserves genealogies—remember who you are. And Deuteronomy serves as a second summary as the people begin to move into this land that will also become so closely associated with their identity. Those five books help the children of Israel remember who they are and whose they are. And while, of course, the stories had been passed down orally and some had even been written down before, this was a concerted effort to preserve their story so that it would not be lost in the Diaspora, the exile, or in any other time of trial that might follow.

The Silents lived under the pressure of the Cold War for most of their adult lives. Then, when the Cold War faded away, it was replaced by increasing acts of terrorism that threatened our way of life. Is it any wonder that the Silents as a whole are a conservative group? They have spent their lives trying to hold on to the American identity that

PROPHETS TO THE GENERATIONS

brought everyone such hope through World War II and the prosperous 1950s.[8] It was during the early adulthood of the Silents that "In God we trust" was added to our currency, and "under God" was added to the Pledge of Allegiance. The Silent Generation views God and country as both worth preserving, a perspective that stems from their own very real experiences of threats to these two things. It is as if they are living in their own exile and just want something that has meaning for them to hold on to. It is not malicious or condescending; it is simply their way of holding on to the things that give them comfort.

It reminds me of an experience I had early in my ministry at one of the churches I have served. There had been a movement among the younger generations to remove the flags from the sanctuary. In fact, some of them simply moved it and hoped it would go unnoticed. It did not go unnoticed by one of the Silents in my congregation. He came to me very upset that it was gone. At first, I tried to reason with him and explain how younger generations see the flag in the sanctuary as implying that we worship America over, or at least as much as, God. The man wouldn't budge. So, I asked him why it was so important to him. He shared that he had an older brother who served in World War II. That brother never came home. The devastation to him

---

[8] Of course, we now acknowledge that life was not great for everyone in that time period. Minorities and women continued to be excluded, infantilized, and restricted from full participation in society. See, for example, the denial of the GI Bill to African American soldiers. A program that lifted the white middle class tremendously simultaneously barred the African American community from access to that same prosperity.

and his parents was nearly unbearable. He explained that the flag, when placed in the worship space, symbolized all the saints who had gone before—and for him, it meant he was still worshiping alongside his brother. He didn't want the flag anywhere near the altar, because he agrees that we don't worship our country over or even equal to God. He just wanted the flag there so his brother and all those lost in all the wars are still remembered and included.

So, we have the flag in the corner of the sanctuary. We also have a contemporary worship space that has no flags at all.

The Silents have a lot of life experience to share, and they have some anxiety about what has been lost. The same was true for the people of the exile in Isaiah. When the Silents look around, they see almost nothing of their childhood still with us. Those who were set to return home from the exile had likely never lived in that homeland before. All of it would be strange to them, too. In those moments, we hold on to prophetic hope—that even when things change, God remains steadfast.

May we see in Isaiah and in the Silents' steadfast perspective that very hope as well. And may we recognize, in the long histories of Isaiah and the Silents, the persistence of life with God through all things.

Discussion Questions:

1. How do Isaiah and the Silent Generation illustrate the value of perseverance and hope in times of national trauma and change?

2. What are the strengths and challenges of working for justice "from within the system" as Isaiah and many Silents did?

3. How does the idea of God being present "in the wilderness" shift our understanding of divine presence in times of exile or dislocation?

4. In what ways does societal migration—from rural to urban—continue to affect spiritual identity and religious expression today?

5. What can younger generations learn from the Silent Generation's approach to memory, loss, and tradition in their faith practices?

Martin Luther King, Jr.

We will see a pattern that the prophets who spoke to and spoke out the worldviews of the generation they shaped often come from the generation before them, and King is no exception. Though a member of the Silent Generation, King was anything but silent. While many people would stand out as voices calling for social change (Malcolm X, Medgar Evers, Gloria Steinem, Harvey Milk), King rises above all of them, remaining a clarion call to this day. His "I Have a Dream" speech at the March on Washington casts a prophetic vision of a world that could be—and, in part, is—thanks to his words and the movement he energized. He is also a good reminder of the prophetic risk of standing against the powers and principalities. Although he paid the ultimate price with his life, his work and words live on and continue to shape our world today.

CHAPTER THREE
Jeremiah and the Boomers
(b. 1945-1964)

Why pair Jeremiah and the Boomers? Is it because "Jeremiah was a bullfrog, He was a good friend of mine"[9]? As on-the-nose as that song may be, this pairing has more to do with the ridiculous optimism of both the prophet and the generation of Boomers, those born between 1945 and 1964. Both Jeremiah and the Boomers start their lives in times of tremendous prosperity, but as time rolls on, that prosperity faces significant challenges. The prophet and the generation rise to the occasion, even as they voiced their discontent. They hold on to their optimism, even as they complain about the impact on their personal lives.

But let's put both in their historical context to understand how these seemingly contradictory stances can coexist. Jeremiah begins his commission during the reign of King Josiah. Of all the kings described in the history of the two kingdoms of Israel and Judah, Josiah is arguably the most notable. Josiah restored the centrality of the Law and clearly worked to define the people as the kind of followers God seeks. Yet despite Josiah's greatness, he still meets a

---

[9] Hoyt Axton, "Joy to the World," performed by Three Dog Night, on *Naturally*, ABC/ Dunhill Records, 1970, LP.

cold end. He was killed in battle at Megiddo while trying
to stop Pharaoh Neco of Egypt, despite the warnings not
to interfere. Josiah's death marks the great downturn in
Judah's history. From that point on, it is a steady march
to dysfunction and exile. Yet despite that shift, Jeremiah
remains optimistic about the days to come. He, however,
also personally carries the burden of the fall of Jerusalem,
narrating much of that portion of Israel's history in terms of
his own life story.

The Boomers were also born in a time of tremendous
prosperity. Born following the end of World War II, they
stepped into a world where the United States had become
the dominant cultural and political force. They are also
called the Boomers because the birth rate rose sharply
in the twenty years marking their generation (recall
that the birth control pill became widely available in the
mid-1960s, marking the end of the boom). The combination
of widespread prosperity and the need to build to
accommodate the boom of babies meant that everywhere
the Boomers went, new things greeted them: new hospitals,
new schools, new houses, and so on. The affluence and
the newness of the world created the optimism of this
generation, as well as the self-centeredness.[10] Television and
the move to the cities and suburbs caused this generation
to question the values of their parents at a rate never before
seen among generations.[11] They deliberately took prophetic

---

[10] Haydn Shaw, *Sticking Points*, 72-76, 81.

[11] Haydn Shaw, *Sticking Points*, 77-80.

roles, actively trying to shape society to reflect their values. While some of the prophetic figures were Silents (i.e., Martin Luther King Jr.), Boomers provided the youthful and collective energy that would propel movements like civil rights, gender rights, and disability rights forward. Where Jeremiah's people were forced into exile, the Boomers sought to exile the outdated values of their parents. Yet now they face the disappointment of not having actually completed that work, and some of them express bitterness as they have become the people to be resisted.

With those characteristics in mind, let's look deeper at the complicated but ultimately hopeful prophet and generation.

Live Long and Prosper

There is nothing like a safe and prosperous childhood to set your worldview on an optimistic note. Jeremiah and the Boomers both lay claim to that reality. As mentioned, Jeremiah began during the reign of Josiah, and the Boomers emerged during the post-war boom.

Jeremiah prefers to be a prophet of hope rather than one of gloom and doom. Even though Jeremiah is also the purported author of Lamentations, there are three instances in Jeremiah's prophetic career that underscore his optimism. First, there is his willingness to be convinced not to deliver the prophecy of doom in Chapter 28. When the other (false) prophets deliver news to the king that they will be successful at holding off their invaders,

Jeremiah—who was directed by God to deliver the opposite prophecy, represented by the wooden yoke around his neck—agrees with the others and breaks the wooden yoke. Unfortunately for Jeremiah, God sends him back, this time with an iron yoke that cannot be broken.

Another optimistic moment in Jeremiah's career occurs with the announcement of the new covenant in Chapter 31. Just a couple of chapters prior to that one, Jeremiah speaks the Lord's word, one of the most hopeful verses in the entire Bible, 29:11: "I know the plans I have in mind for you, declares the Lord; they are plans for peace, not disaster, to give you a future filled with hope." The striking reality is that both that promise and the New Covenant are established when the Babylonian army successfully sieges Jerusalem.

The prophet Jeremiah also personally invests in that hope in this third moment of his career. While he sits in jail, a kinsman comes to sell him a field. Jeremiah knows this field is about to fall into the hands of Babylon, and he will be exiled far away from it, and yet he agrees to buy the field anyway. Why? Because he truly believes in God's promise and knows that he will one day reclaim that field, even if it is actually his heirs who do so.

The Boomers have also taken a generously optimistic view of life, even as they worked to challenge the old idea of the American dream that was not as inclusive as it could be. Part of that optimism came from the prosperity around them. Part of it came from the reality that the world all seemed new as they rose through the ranks.[12] Combine that with the hints of greater equality that had happened before their birth in World War II—the service of African American men[13] and Rosie the Riveter entering the workforce—and they saw before them enormous possibilities for what the world could be.

Those visions of greater equality were marked not only by significant movements such as the Civil Rights Movement and the Equal Rights Amendment (ERA), but they were also reflected in the pop culture of the day. Gene Roddenberry created such a world in Star Trek. While it was not particularly popular in its initial run, it did include significant representation, notably with Lieutenant Uhura, played by Nichelle Nichols. The plots frequently pushed for a more utopian vision, and the series included the first interracial kiss on scripted television between Uhura and Captain Kirk.[14] While the actors were all of the Silent Generation, pop culture was squarely being aimed at the Boomers, who were the largest marketing block the world had ever seen. Television had to reflect the values of this up-and-coming generation to hold its attention.

---

[12] Haydn Shaw, *Sticking Points*, 72-74.

[13] Black men had served in prior wars as well, but with each war that included them, the more the movement shifted toward fuller inclusion. Plus, it was the Boomers and the Silents who would push for the amendment to the Constitution that would lower the voting age to eighteen. One of the key points that was made for that amendment argued that if eighteen-year-olds could be drafted and die in war, they should also have a voice in electing the leaders who decide whether the nation goes to war. Military service, then, was a key building block in the efforts of inclusion.

[14] "Plato's Stepchildren," *Star Trek*, Season 3, Episode 10. Aired November 22, 1968, on NBC.

Of course, both Jeremiah and the Boomers would find it was not so simple as proclaiming a New Covenant for the people. The reality of making that transition came with great sacrifice, and it required full commitment of the prophets to make it happen. It also meant more than just talking the talk. Walking the walk, no matter how difficult it was, would be a necessity for change.

Sitting in a Well and a Drugstore

Prophetic acts and images are crucial to the work of a prophet. Such works give a visual reality to convey choices, morality, lessons, and warnings. Both Jeremiah and the Boomers relied on such actions to carry their message.

We have already discussed a couple of such acts in Jeremiah's story: the yoke and the field. The yoke, turned from wood to iron, carried the prophetic warning of the impending doom that Judah would face at the hands of the Babylonians. However, all would not be lost. Jeremiah knew that the Lord would bring them home again one day. Jeremiah invested in that hope when he bought the field that he himself might never use or enjoy.

Jeremiah's call story, recounted in the first chapter, contains additional prophetic actions. First, as the Lord anoints Jeremiah, the Lord touches Jeremiah's mouth and tells him, "I'm putting my words in your mouth" (Jer 1:9b). Then, through visions, the Lord actually gives Jeremiah two images to foretell what is coming: an almond tree, which represents God watching over to fulfill God's word, and a pot boiling over from the north, which represents the coming Babylonian army (Jer 1:11-14). Symbolic acts shape him from the very beginning of Jeremiah's work as a prophet.

Another event in Jeremiah's narrative represents the state of the people, although it is framed simply as punishment for the prophet's damning predictions. In an attempt to rid himself of Jeremiah and his meddling, King Zedekiah has Jeremiah thrown into a well, where he is expected to starve or sink to his death. Later, Ebed-melech (the Ethiopian court official) advocates for him, and Jeremiah is moved to prison instead. Jeremiah's own life story is representative of the people, who will at first go through a siege that will devastate the population from being unable to flee, and some will die of starvation before there is a surrender that will preserve the people, though they will be in captivity. The prophet is as the people are. There can be no doubt that as the people experience their muck, the image of the prophet will come to mind.

Images of suffering are difficult to throw off. As the Boomers began to confront the inequalities of society, the images projected on television and into the homes of ordinary Americans proved crucial to changing society. From police dogs and hoses turned on Black children to the horrors of Vietnam, the images on the television screen forced people to ask whether this was the kind of society they wanted to live in. For many, the answer was no. Actions forced them, however, to confront questions they had been able to deny otherwise.

Other actions were taken deliberately to force retrospection as well. Think of the Montgomery bus boycott. The March to Selma. The March on Washington. Sit-ins at diners and drug stores. Burning bras. While these were actions that both Silents and Boomers had a hand in orchestrating, to the American public, it was the participation of the youth that compelled real change in the minds of the people. The Boomers were collectively engaging in prophetic work.

First-Person Perspective

The ironic aspect of the Boomers' collective work to change the world is that they soon settled into the status quo and became great defenders of it. The Baby Boomers are also known as "The Me Generation." The Boomers face a significant challenge in part due to their sheer numbers and the initial success of opening up society (in this case, the workforce) to so many others, namely, competition for jobs. As they moved past their idealistic youth, they had to face the responsibility of providing for a family. They have also spent their whole lives fighting to be noticed in a giant generation. As they achieved some of the changes they had set out to make collectively, they turned back to focusing on achieving success as individuals.[15] The peace-loving hippies became the Gordon Gekko character from the 1987 film *Wall Street*, proclaiming, "Greed, for lack of a better word, is good!"[16]

---

[15] Hadyn Shaw, *Sticking Points*, 73-75.

[16] *Wall Street*, directed by Oliver Stone (Los Angeles: 20th Century Fox, 1987), film.

As a book, Jeremiah reads less like a collective narrative of a whole people than a first-person story that is used to represent a people. The rhetorical result, then, is that Jeremiah is elevated in importance as well. Much of the narrative is told in first person, making the story all about Jeremiah. Even as he insists he is representing the people, this is Jeremiah's story more than anything else.

This is a danger of the prophetic role. A prophet is only successful if people are paying attention to the individual making these claims. Jeremiah is no exception, and the narrative's structure underscores this truth. As a generation, the Boomers have always had the world's attention. Is it any wonder that they became so self-focused once they felt they succeeded at the changes they sought to make? That individualism paid off incredibly well for them. This is the generation of summer homes and more vehicles than family members. The field they invested in way back has turned into dividends. But have they lost sight of their commission to collective justice in the meantime?

Never Coming Home

Another frustrating aspect of prophetic work is that you rarely see the full realization of the hopeful vision you cast. It truly depends on when you show up in the narrative. Jeremiah may have purchased a field, but the exile would continue for more than seventy years. If Jeremiah made it back, it would have been a miracle. Perhaps that implicit knowledge is why he is associated with Lamentations. That author took deep complaints to God, complaints that things are not changing as fast as the prophet wants them to change.

But what if Jeremiah had made it back? He would have returned in his retirement era as one of the landowners. Such ownership at the very least meant that he would have returned to prosperity. It might also have meant that he had the right to displace people who were living there and lay claim to what was his. He would have been one of the landed aristocracy, so to speak. Instead of challenging the status quo, he would have become the status quo.

This is the charge that younger generations now level at the Boomers. In a recent talk uploaded to YouTube by *WSJ (Wall Street Journal) News,* New York University professor of marketing Scott Galloway, himself a Boomer, talks about the economic disadvantages that younger generations are truly facing today. For the first time in our recent history, thirty-year-olds are significantly worse off than their parents. This is due, in large part, to the control the Boomer generation—America's wealthiest generation of all time—has on our economy.

Galloway levels a significant charge at his own industry—academia—for continuing to consolidate wealth in the older population, undermining opportunities for our youth to flourish. During his talk, he explains that he returns all of his compensation from NYU in an attempt to balance the scales, a recognition that, within the Boomer generation, there is still a desire to change the world for the better.[17] As younger generations confront the problems of today, it is good to remember that the Boomers (and some late Silents) led the charge in some of the more radical shifts in our society—shifts that many benefit from today.

In general, however, the Boomers have shifted from being the people of resistance to being the people to be resisted. They may have significantly orchestrated a change in American society, but their work was incomplete. There is still racial inequality in representation across society. Women entered the workforce, but at bargain-basement prices that have not yet been equalized. The Americans with Disabilities Act was passed, but initially, it expanded services that kept people with disabilities isolated from regular society (the proverbial short bus comes to mind). And while the Silents broke open the conversation about LGBTQIA+ rights with the Stonewall riots, AIDS prompted the Boomers, who were in positions of influence by that time, to justify discrimination in the name of world health. And then, to add insult to injury, another generation as large as they are showed up with new idealism and prophetic proclamations, and their cries of damnation were directed at the Boomers. They would use technology to boil the whole generation down to a meme: "Ok, Boomer." In the next chapter, we will discuss how that generation carried on the work of the Boomers, while

---

[17] "Scott Galloway Describes the Tough Future Facing Gen Z," *WSJ News,* https://www.youtube.com/watch?v=tFk5gGbSBas&list=PLxB23mVwj7uxTElEAe5dFjEmbhOuOy0SY&index=6.

simultaneously cutting ties with them.

And thus is the heartbreaking work of any prophet. You may live long enough to prosper, to see your words become a new reality. But you may also live long enough to become the system you once resisted. It would do us all some good to have a bit of humility about that. The cyclical nature of history tends to make us all heroes and villains. Or perhaps it is more accurate to say it makes us all prophets and prophecy.

Discussion Questions:

1. What parallels can you draw between Jeremiah's personal suffering and the generational shifts experienced by the Boomers?

2. How does prosperity in one's youth shape long-term attitudes about change, justice, and risk?

3. In what ways can prophetic action become co-opted by the very systems it once resisted?

4. How does media—ancient and modern—serve as a tool for prophecy and social change?

5. What are the responsibilities of a generation that has "lived long enough to become the status quo"?

Beyoncé Knowles and Kendrick Lamar

The Millennial Generation might best be characterized as the generation that democratized voice. They are the generation of social media, but also a generation that has been able to access and popularize music outside the constraints of industry powerhouses. While Beyoncé certainly benefited from the industry through her work with Destiny's Child, both she and Kendrick Lamar have been able to define their music around their heritage and artistry, as people can access what they write. They have significantly called for the Black experience to be as valid as the white experience, and Beyoncé has critiqued gender assumptions in her work as well ("Run the World [Girls]" and "Single Ladies" are two popular examples). Both artists drew criticism and controversy with their Super Bowl performances, which, in turn, inspired collective reflection on race and prejudice in the United States. They make us think. And then they make at least some of us seek to do better. That is the work of a prophet.

CHAPTER FOUR
Ezekiel and the Millennials
(1981-1996)

The Participant Trophy Generation

The Avocado Toast Generation

The Locally Sourced Generation

The Social Media Generation

These are the supposedly derisive terms used to describe Millennials. Mostly these days, Millennials spend less time objecting to their moniker and more time trying to distinguish themselves from the darker, more skeptical generation that comes after them (more on Gen Z in the next chapter). Despite all the hate leveled at this generation, they generally continue to exhibit some of the idealism and optimism of their youth, which was prevalent during the prosperous and positive 1980s and 1990s.

Still, Millennials have lived through some weird days. They have just managed to stay hopeful within themselves. Enter the prophet Ezekiel. Ezekiel definitely undertakes some weird prophetic actions. He also shares some terrifying visions and words of condemnation for the nations. Yet more than one-third of the book, Chapters 33-48, are ultimately very hopeful proclamations, something that is odd for a people experiencing an exile from their homeland. The exiled people carry with them a vision of what could be, because they still remember what was. Wait, which exiled people am I talking about, the people of Ezekiel's time, or the Millennial generation of now? Both, as we shall see.

A Generation of Before and During

Many of the prophets we encounter in this study are adjacent to exile. The Jewish people underwent two significant exiles: the Assyrian Exile of the Northern Kingdom of Israel in 732 BCE and the Babylonian Exile of the Southern Kingdom of Judah in 587 BCE. These are such world-altering events that the prophets who either warned of the coming invasions or called for repentance and/or offered hope in light of these invasions are remembered and canonized. Ezekiel did both. He is honest about the destruction of the Babylonian invasion and the price paid for disobedience, but he also makes a quick turn to offer hope on the other side of that invasion. As has already been mentioned, roughly a third of the book reflects a hopeful vision for what is yet to come for these exiled people. That is somewhat remarkable, considering Ezekiel appears to have been written just before and in the early years of the Babylonian Exile. That level of hope, emerging so early in the exile, is remarkable.

The Millennial Generation experienced childhood in the 1980s and 1990s. They get their name because many of them came of adult age at the turn of the millennium. Like their

Boomer parents who grew up in the 1950s, Millennials experienced a childhood of great prosperity and optimism. They were imbued with that optimism as well. Millennials, encouraged and nurtured to believe in themselves through active campaigns for their self-esteem (such as participant trophies), had an idealism instilled in them that is largely still present even as they confront an adulthood marked by more struggles. Yes, they entered adulthood just as the world wrestled with Y2K, America was under attack on 9/11, and the economy bottomed out in 2008-2009. However, many of them also voted for the first time in a presidential election where a man of color campaigned using the hopeful slogan, "Yes, We Can!" Probably not coincidentally, the elder Millennials were raising children, and the younger Millennials were children who were watching Bob the Builder also proclaim, "Can we fix it? Yes, we can!"

What Millennials and Ezekiel share is confronting challenging days with a memory of how things used to be. And things were that way, really, just a few years ago. Both the prophet and the generation know what is possible, and they are convinced they can get back to those days. Or perhaps it is better put that they believe we can move toward days even better than the past.

There may be no more hopeful image for both the prophet and this generation, no better passage that reflects that optimism of possibility, than the Valley of Dry Bones in Ezekiel 37. God and Ezekiel survey a valley covered with bones. Not just bones. Dry bones. There is no possibility for life in those bones, and yet that is the question that God poses to Ezekiel: "Can these bones live again?" Ezekiel's response is one of possibility, not fully understanding what could be, but at least being open to hope: "Lord God, only you know." As the passage unfolds, however, it is not solely God who brings the bones to life. God invites Ezekiel to speak prophecy and bring the bones to life, which he does.

Both the prophet and the generation have an image of possibility. No matter how dark the days get, there is always hope. Better days are just around the corner; they can feel it. Of course, those days won't come unless they do their part. They are the key to the change actually happening.

Prophets Gone Viral

Ezekiel is not just responsible for dry bones walking around. In fact, if you are familiar at all with a prophet doing something weird to get people's attention, you are probably thinking about Ezekiel (another possibility is Elisha, but he is in a history book, not a prophetic book). Let's take a look at the weird things Ezekiel does:

- Builds a miniature siege of Jerusalem (Ezekiel 4:1-3)

- Lies on his side for over a year (left side for 390 days, right side for 40 days) to symbolize the years of sin of the two kingdoms (4:4-8)

- Eats food cooked over dung to represent life in exile (4:9-12)

PROPHETS TO THE GENERATIONS

- Shaves his head and beard, an action forbidden to priests, and divides it into thirds to burn part of it, strike part with the sword, and throw part to the wind, to represent what will happen to people as a result of conquest (5:1-4)

- Carries his belongings through a hole in the wall to enact the exile and the failed escape of Judah's king (12:1-7)

- Refuses to mourn his wife's death in solidarity with the lack of time for mourning during the siege and exile (24:15-27)

- Becomes mute twice, only able to speak once God speaks (3:26-27; 24:27)

Each of these individual actions is intended to capture the attention of the people and try to turn them from their ways, or at least allow them to prepare for what is coming. But the only way these things work as messages is if people are watching. Because of Ezekiel's position as a priest, people would be watching, but there had to be more at work. Word of mouth had to spread and cause people to watch him. In a sense, Ezekiel was a social media prophet. He went viral as more and more people shared his symbolic actions through word of mouth.

Millennials were the last generation to grow up without social media in their childhoods. True, the very youngest of them were still kids when Facebook was invented, but remember that the social networking site began as a platform only available to college kids. Even as other social media platforms emerged, the majority of Millennials had cleared childhood before they had access to such things. Also, a majority of social media platform founders have thus far been Millennials, including those who founded Facebook, Instagram, and Snapchat (MySpace and Twitter were predominantly founded by Gen Xers).

Millennials, then, primarily experienced the benefits of social media, rather than its drawbacks. They avoided the bullying tactics or, at least, were subject to them when they had the maturity to disregard such things or access to mental health professionals to help them process such attacks. Filters have largely been a tool that Gen Z has had to deal with, so the unrealistic expectations that social media can generate have also had minimal effect on Millennials. Since they spent their childhoods without smartphones and social media, they still know how to build community without technology. Late Millennials were found to be some of the most socially connected, least isolated teenagers in a thirty-year study.[18]

Millennials dodged the negative aspects of social media while also capitalizing on its positives. They have used social media to take individual stands on issues that have then consequently become widespread movements. As the founders of the majority of social media platforms, Millennials have empowered movements such as the Arab Spring, #MeToo, Black Lives Matter, and Occupy Wall Street,

---

[18] Jean Twenge, *Generations*, 393.

among others. All of these movements, however, got energy from individuals promoting them from their own unique platforms. The collective response of individuals then created social change.

Millennials and Ezekiel align in the assumption that individuals can cause collective change. Whether it is through hashtags or casting your beard to the wind, the goal is the same: get attention to inspire people to turn around and do better. In theological terms, that is called repentance. But maybe theological terms are not the most suitable for this generation, or for this prophet.

God Has Left the Building (And So Did We)

Both Millennials and Ezekiel share another common critique: institutional religion is unnecessary. While Gen X grew up and became less and less interested in organized religion, Millennials are the generation that grew up outside the church in far greater numbers. Their rejection of organized religion reflects their general rejection of institutions. They have either delayed or avoided marriage in far greater numbers, and they prefer locally sourced rather than brand names (more on that in a minute). A rejection of the church aligns with their general *modus operandi* in this sense.

However, turning against an institution that had been so central to much of Western civilization's history was also a bold step, and it is significant how many of them walked away. According to a 2020 survey by the Cooperative

Election Survey, by 2020, the number of Millennials in the U.S. who identified as Christian was almost equal to the number who identified as atheist, agnostic, or none, at 44 percent and 43 percent, respectively.[19] Their generation was the first to reach such a milestone (Gen Z will push it even further). Why do they reject organized religion? In part, it is because it interferes with their individual identity and expression. It also, however, violates some of their own key moral stances. Non-acceptance of LGBTQIA+ people, for instance, is routinely cited by this generation as a reason to reject Christianity. Six out of ten Millennials see religion as too intolerant of others.[20] Millennials might be more interested in Christianity if it actually lived out the values it proclaims, especially love of neighbor.

Ironically, Millennials find soul companions in the prophets. Practically every prophet levels a critique against the people for not seeking justice for the most vulnerable in society and for missing the point of worshiping God, which is not to go through a series of rituals but to take care of people. The prophets also have to wrestle with the reality of conquest, which results in the destruction of the Temple and causes a genuine faith crisis for the people. How are they supposed to worship God if they have nowhere to go to worship?

Ezekiel is no exception to this prophetic work. He calls out the idolatry that has offended God (Chapter 8), then

---

[19] Jean Twenge, *Generations*, 298.

[20] Jean Twenge, *Generations*, 301.

watches God's glory leave the Temple (Chapters 9-11). What is striking about Ezekiel in comparison to other prophets is that he is a priest (Ezekiel 1:3)! Someone who should have been all in on the work of the Temple and devastated by God's abandonment of it, instead finds meaning in continuing to deliver God's words outside the Temple.

Neither Ezekiel nor Millennials[21] have given up on God. They both just recognize and call out circumstances that may justify the rejection of organized religion. Those of us who remain in the church would do well to listen to the critique. We should keep our churches and religious practices in line with what we believe about God. When those things are out of alignment, some dismantling should happen. But lest we feel personally attacked, it is good for us to remember that we aren't the only institution core to American identity that Millennials and prophets are challenging. Another institution often behaves like a religion: capitalism.

Heart of Stone

My best friend, Rev. James Kjorlaug, is a Millennial. When we like to get under each other's skin, we give each other a hard time about our generations. One of his favorite ways to deride me is to accuse me of being obsessed with chain restaurants and their giant, ecologically damaging parking lots. I come right back at him and say, "At least I

---

[21] Despite a drop in church attendance or adherence to Christianity, a majority of Millennials still believe in God and pray from time to time. See Jean Twenge, *Generations*, 301.

can park less than five miles from the place we are trying to eat, and at least my restaurants seat more than five people total." His obsession with local places that use locally sourced food and disrupt the mass market and publicly traded big business drives my generation—Gen X, raised on commercials and common national goods—a little crazy.

But then I think about his tattoo.

James has half a tattoo sleeve on one of his arms depicting a heart that is half in vibrant color and half in stark outline on bare skin. The inspiration comes from this verse: "I will give you a new heart and put a new spirit in you. I will remove your stony heart from your body and replace it with a heart of flesh" (Ezekiel 36:26). The half of the tattoo that is in vibrant color is actually a heart shaped like a cut gemstone. James argues that a heart of stone must be something beautiful, seductive, something we would want to hold on to and resist releasing. There must be a reason why we stubbornly refuse to adopt the more authentic, living, and loving heart that God wants us to have.

James' heart tattoo echoes for me his generation's longing to reject large-scale capitalism. It comes from a place of real hurt. The economy has not been a safe place for Millennials. Many of them entered the workforce right as the economy tanked in 2007-2008. The younger ones of them watched their parents lose jobs as a result. Additionally, many of them still carry student loans for college that have not been paid off yet. They struggle to afford houses in this new economy and generally feel betrayed by capitalism.[22]

So, in response, Millennials have actively worked to dismantle capitalism. They were instrumental in organizing Occupy Wall Street and supported Bernie Sanders for President in significant numbers. They support and start local businesses, and are more likely than any other generation to choose to live as minimalists. Marie Kondo, herself a Millennial minimalist and coiner of the phrase, "Does it spark joy?" is a good example.

Millennials, as a generation, are seeking that heart of flesh Ezekiel calls us to have. They are trying to find meaning in experiences and in healthy working boundaries, choosing to work to live rather than live to work.[23] All the critiques leveled against them—avocado toast, social media, participant trophies, and locally sourced—don't seem like terrible things once we understand them as reflections of key values. Whether we agree with their choices or not, we can see how they came to make them. We can also hear within them the prophetic voice.

Ezekiel contains elements, like the vision of the many beasts and the wheel in the sky in Chapter 1, that proclaim a new way of being is coming. The world is on the verge

---

[22] Jean Twenge, *Generations*. Twenge remarks that when you look at the numbers, Millennials are actually pretty well off economically (259-267). However, both Twenge and Shaw share that, significant to the Millennial narrative, they feel poor (Twenge, 267-276; Shaw, 114-116). Also, Millennials may be in pretty good economic situations now because they have adopted minimalist lifestyles.

[23] Haydn Shaw, *Sticking Points*, 307-309.

of turning upside down. The prophet is participating in the proclamation of the apocalypse. He finds a true companion in the Millennial generation. They, too, lay the foundation for the world to turn over, whether through the creation of social media, the empowerment of individuals, or the challenge to the dominance of institutions. But Ezekiel is not an apocalyptic book, nor are the Millennials a truly apocalyptic generation. But just such a prophet and just such a generation are on the horizon.

Discussion Questions:

1. How do Ezekiel's prophetic actions parallel the way Millennials use social media to raise awareness and demand change?

2. What does the Valley of Dry Bones story reveal about the power of imagination and hope during times of collapse?

3. Why do you think Millennials have such strong skepticism toward institutions like the Church and capitalism, and how should those institutions respond?

4. How does the Ezekiel 36 vision of a new heart relate to the Millennial generation's value system of minimalism, authenticity, and justice?

5. What are the potential dangers and strengths of rooting social transformation in individual action, as both Ezekiel and Millennials do?

Gen Z Prophets

Malala Yousafzai and Greta Thunberg

These young women are prophets to the generation to which they belong (Malala was born on the cusp between Millennials and Gen Z), marking a shift in culture in which younger and younger people can now be heard. Shot in the head on a bus in Pakistan, Malala Yousafzai became a target of the Pakistani Taliban because she actively campaigned for education rights for girls in her home region of Swat. The fight for her life and subsequent survival only amplified her prophetic voice. Greta Thunberg began striking from school to convince her home country of Sweden to align with the Paris climate agreement. She spoke before the United Nations, urging the countries of the world to take the climate crisis seriously, calling them out for their collective negligence in what became known as her "How Dare You!" speech. Her generation has always faced the threat of the world coming to an end, and she gives voice and fights against such doom. Both girls were nominated for the Nobel Peace Prize before the age of 18, with Malala winning in 2014 at the age of 17, becoming the youngest Nobel Laureate in history. These two young women have shown that prophetic work has no age limit. Anyone can speak up and help change God's world for the better.

CHAPTER FIVE
Daniel and Gen Z
(b. 1997-2012)

"Shouldn't we do something?!" my ten-year-old son exclaimed. We were just sitting in front of the television as a family, watching a show, when he lost it unexpectedly.

Confused, I responded, "What?"

"Shouldn't we do something?!?!?"

"No, I heard you. What do you mean? What should we be doing?"

"Something! Anything! I mean, the world is coming to an end in, like, a month, and we are just sitting here watching TV!"

I should tell you this scene took place in November of 2012. As he so eloquently put it, the world was predicted to come to an end, thanks to the Mayan calendar, in, like, a month—specifically, December 21, 2012.

"Oh, honey," I replied, "Don't worry about that. This is just your first end of the world."

I have thought back on that conversation often and recognized how much it represents a Gen Z worldview intersecting with the good old nonchalant sarcasm of a

Gen Xer. You will learn more about Xers in the next chapter. Here, though, we now encounter the generation that is very appropriately named Gen Z, because theirs is the generation where everything comes to an end.

Thankfully, they have a prophet who can walk alongside them in Daniel, our one and only apocalyptic prophet—an apocalypse prophet for an apocalypse generation: a match made in heaven.

The Apocalypse Generation (Sorry, Millennials), The Apocalypse Prophet (Sorry, Ezekiel)

Millennials are often quick to point out that they came into the workforce during the economic downturn of 2008-2009. They will tell us how deeply that impacted their ability to buy a house and save for retirement. The generation that follows them just stares blankly and thinks, "Okay, Karen, go complain to the manager of the space-time continuum." Yes, it is true that it was a hard time to enter the workforce. But what if that was a hard time to enter into existence, period? Gen Z was born in the shadow of 9/11, watched their parents lose their jobs in that 2008-2009 economic downturn, went through the stress of the 2012 Mayan calendar apocalypse at an age when they were just forming their worldviews, watched the nation tear itself to shreds over an incredibly divisive 2016 presidential election around their high school days, went through a literal worldwide apocalypse in the COVID-19 pandemic when they were graduating high school or college, and then watched a repeat of another chaotic presidential election in 2024. And yes, Millennials have been alive through all of this as well, as have Gen X, Boomers, and the Silent Generation. The difference between Gen Z and the others, though, is that Gen Z has only lived through apocalypses. They have no memory of anything else. The world has been crumbling around them for their entire lives.

Daniel, then, is the perfect prophet to match with them. There are only two books in the Bible that are wholly classified as apocalypses: Daniel and Revelation. Other books, including those of other prophets and portions of Jesus' preaching in the Gospels, have apocalyptic elements but do not qualify as apocalypses altogether. Apocalypses describe world-ending events, with the goal of orienting everything around the reign of God (at least in a Judeo-Christian frame). Apocalyptic literature reckons with a reality that is so broken that radical change is necessary. Such literature casts the world in very dualistic terms of good versus evil. Ultimately, good will prevail, but it is an utter disaster to get there.

The Book of Daniel is apocalyptic because it reveals significant breakdowns between those who have power and those who do not, yet those without power predominantly prevail because they are right. Daniel also includes visions, some of which are difficult to interpret. Finally, at the heart of the book is a long description of the Son of Man (Ch. 10). This figure is clearly a supernatural figure who will right the world. The injustice of the world will be countered and overthrown by this figure.

Gen Z needs to see a vision beyond the mess they have known. The way they behave often stems from their efforts to achieve that vision. Other generations would do well to put on their glasses and imagine what it would be like to never know a country that wasn't divided and in crisis. How would you behave? And wouldn't you seek an opportunity to flee into another world, like the ones generated by AI, to escape this one if it was all you knew? The hearers of Daniel needed a new vision of the world to have hope. So does Gen Z. Let them dream. They just might rebuild the world.

Necessary Skills

In one of the first stories of Daniel, Daniel argues with the chief official on behalf of himself and his companions, Hananiah, Mishael, and Azariah (also known as Belteshazzar, Shadrach, Meshach, and Abednego), that they do not need to adhere to the prescribed diet in order to perform their work well. Instead, they can subsist on a vegetarian diet and do just fine. The chief official resists Daniel's plan but finally agrees to it for a limited time. If their work doesn't suffer, then they can keep their diet. If it does, they will have to adhere to the diet of the empire. At the end of the ten-day test, they are doing better than others on the prescribed diet, so they are allowed to do things their way (Dan 1:8-17).

I struggled to teach my son some traditional skills. He does not know how to tie his shoes or ride a bicycle. He was almost twenty years old before he learned to drive. Each attempt at trying to teach him has been met with the same question: "Why do I need to know how to do this?" I will admit, I did not have a good answer for the ones he has never learned to do. My answer was simply, "This is a skill you just need to know." He disagreed. He pointed out that Vans were his favorite shoes, and they slip on. If he needed running shoes, he could always find an option that used Velcro instead of laces, which he argued didn't have the challenge of coming untied all the time.

As for riding a bicycle, none of his friends rode bicycles. Sidewalks were inconsistent in the towns where we lived. It was an ineffective mode of transportation. Plus, he didn't really need transportation in general anyway. He could text his friends, and they could meet up online to play video games. Throughout my son's elementary and secondary school education, he spent only four nights at friends' houses. For the same reason, he didn't learn to drive. Anywhere he needed to go, one of his parents would take him. In the meantime, he didn't have to worry about gas, insurance, or risk.[24] He only eventually learned to drive because he got a job.

Gen Z is not just asking questions about why things are the way they are; they are flat-out refusing to participate in things that just don't make sense anymore. Perhaps this is why interest in college education is dropping among

---

[24] Gen Z has an outsized interest in staying safe. See Jean Twenge, *Generations*, 384-88.

this generation. According to a 2025 article from *Forbes*, 75 percent of Gen Zers believe there are better ways of getting an education than a college degree. The disconnect is a result of two factors: college costs are too high to justify, and college does not actually train people for the workforce.[25] Most of education is still operating as if Google doesn't exist, training people to memorize facts instead of equipping them with skills. This reality, alongside the pressure from AI, may be why so many in Generation Z are opting for trade schools or seeking employment immediately after high school rather than attending college.

Like the four young men in Daniel who pushed back at "But we've always done it this way," Gen Z has little patience for outdated practices. They will just do otherwise. Perhaps their lack of patience is framed by their apocalyptic worldviews. They don't have time to mess around. Unless you can give them a good reason for why things are the way they are, they are just choosing ways in response to what reality actually is now. Don't think you can push them to do otherwise. They will push back. Hard.

Willing to Die for "Live and Let Live"

If there is one defining value of Gen Z, one that collectively brings out their resistant, revolutionary spirit, it is trying to force them to be something they are not. I am not talking about resisting labels. That is a Gen X characteristic,

---

[25] Mark C. Perna, "New Data Reveals Just How Deep the College Crisis Goes," *Forbes*, January 28, 2025, https://www.forbes.com/sites/markcperna/2025/01/28/new-data-reveals-the-depth-of-college-crisis/.

not a Gen Z one. Gen Z wears labels proudly, specifically the labels of identity. Other generations may be irritated by the declaration of their pronouns, but not only does that tell us something important about how they view themselves, it is also a way for them to support others who are defining their identity in a myriad of ways.

Expression of their identity is a do-or-die issue for Gen Z. It is part of how they lay claim to better mental health. It is also a litmus test for them about how accepting others are. Gen Z has zero tolerance for intolerance. In fact, it might even be put stronger. They have zero tolerance for not being fully accepted. This is the generation raised on the ease of protest, whether it is marching in the streets or changing your profile picture on social media. They live their values out loud. They also have very little room for gray in their worldview—you either accept or you don't. You are either someone they will talk to and engage with, or you are not. It's no surprise that an apocalyptic generation casts things in such stark, good-versus-evil extremes.

While it is true that Gen Z has more atheists than any other generation, many still identify as Christian. For this group, when they insist on the acceptance of who they are, they are seeking the freedom to be who God has created them to be and for that creation to be honored. This generation of Christians takes the love of God and the love of neighbor seriously, and judgment is not part of that equation. Other generations may bristle against their theology and their demands of acceptance, but let me put a challenge before

67

us. How is that any different than Daniel's willingness to go to the lions' den, or Meshach, Shadrach, and Abednego accepting the punishment of being tossed in a furnace? There was a line that the authorities could not cross for them, and it was the line of being able to worship God in the way that they saw fit. When laws were passed restricting that worship, these four would give their all to protest such intolerance and injustice. Gen Z is just doing the same. They want to be able to proclaim a God who loves all people and practice a faith that reflects that love. They will give their life to that mission.

Speaking in Code

When we did the sermon series that gave rise to this book, I opened worship with a welcome that was loaded down in the slang of the generation we were discussing. Gen Z was the hardest for me to do. I really had very little idea what I was saying. I could get "slay" and "riz," but "cheugy"? Thank God for the Urban Dictionary (if you have never ventured into the Urban Dictionary, enter with caution). But even with the knowledge of what the words meant, it was painful coming from my fifty-year-old mouth. I remember one of my choir members crying out, "Just stop!"

Slang has always distinguished generations. We all have it. It bonds us together in our youth. It is a way of resisting the adult authorities around us. It is another identity-creating force. One of the ways slang is created, or cultivated, is through collective pop culture moments, moments that are shared *en masse* by the generation. Either a pop culture moment happens and that forms the slang, or pop culture helps popularize slang that comes from the streets.

The thing is, because slang comes from or is enforced by pop culture, all the generations have access to that influence. Even though older generations might not use the slang, they at least had access to its origins and thus had a shot at understanding it. But now we are up against a completely different force: the algorithm.

Social media and streaming platforms curate the things we see. Some of this curation keeps the older people from seeing what the young people see. Now there are whole worlds based on not just our political leanings or our interests (who else out there is a fan of stick tok—TikTok videos featuring interesting sticks people have found—yes, that's a thing). Our ages also shape those worlds. So, an entire generation can have a collective pop culture moment that the other generations never see. So Gen Alpha knows where "Skibidi toilet" comes from, and Gen Z knows why being "so Ohio" is an insult, but Gen X and up are completely mystified.

Slang is now a code that is much harder to crack. These generations are speaking a different language right in front of the older generations, and we have no idea what they are saying. I mean, no idea. And we don't even know where to look. Even when we use our electronic devices to crack the code, we still don't get what is going on because it really involves immersing ourselves in a curated world that we barely have access to.

Despite the relatively recent appearance of the algorithm, using coded language is not a new phenomenon. People who are resisting the authorities over them have always come up with ways of communicating things right under the nose of power that power can't comprehend. Apocalyptic literature depends on such coding, and Daniel is no exception. One way apocalypses hide meaning is in visions. Visions depend on symbolism, and symbolism is inherently slippery. When I teach apocalyptic literature, I use the symbol of an eagle as an example. In the first century, depending on who you were and what perspective you had, the eagle could represent Zeus, Caesar, God, or Christ. So if an eagle showed up in Christian literature as a symbol of heroism, Caesar could interpret it as confirmation of his benevolent leadership, while Christians would read it as a hopeful vision of Christ overthrowing Caesar. To use an example I just referred to, someone from the southern part of the U.S. might hear "Ohio" used in derogatory terms and assume it was a critique about northerners, while Gen Z knows better. I don't exactly know what they know, though, because I am Gen X.

Daniel also contains two other language tools of resistance. One is that Daniel 2:4-7:28 is actually written in a different language. Instead of being written in Hebrew, this stretch was written in Aramaic. Why does that matter? It is not that no one in the government knows Aramaic, but rather that far fewer do. Aramaic was the language of the common people, not the scholars and officials. Take note that this stretch of Daniel is where direct opposition to the king occurs. There is a blatant call for resisting unjust powers through these sections, including threats and warnings of the king's ultimate demise.

And which king is being threatened? Nebuchadnezzar of Babylon. This leads to the second example of coded language, because while Daniel is set in the Babylonian Exile, it was actually written about 400 years later during the Maccabean revolt. During that revolt, the Jews successfully overthrew the reign of the Seleucid emperor Antiochus Epiphanes IV when he converted (or tried to convert) the Temple in Jerusalem to a pagan site of emperor worship. Allegedly, a gold statue of the emperor was placed in the Temple. Remember what got Shadrach, Meshach, and Abednego in trouble? They refused to worship the gold statue of Nebuchadnezzar. When Nebuchadnezzar backs off his demand, his kingship is saved. A similar thing happens later in the the story to King Darius over the lions' den moment. However, King Belshazzar refuses to heed such warnings, and the writing is literally on the wall (this is where that expression comes from, by the way), condemning him to die.

The comparison between these stories of the Babylonian Exile and the reality of the Jewish people in revolt is obvious. However, the placement in a different time and at the feet of a different empire gives the revolutionaries enough cover to say, "That's just a story from a different time." The Seleucid Empire might have thought it knew what was being said in this story (which is still in the Aramaic portion, by the way), but they couldn't be sure. Just like the incoherence of algorithm-curated slang, the Jewish people can spread the message of revolution right under the nose of power.

That Took a Turn

While much of the Book of Daniel casts a hopeful vision for living under the pressures of empire, it also works with another significant trait of apocalyptic literature: pessimism about the current reality. Daniel creates a story where there is little trust in the leaders. They are either weak and incompetent, as when the kings and their wise people cannot interpret what are probably fairly easy-to-understand visions, or deliberately violating the rights of their people, as when they insist on infringing upon religion. In the face of such struggles, either Daniel and his friends show themselves to be the wisest or they must face a great threat to their own personal safety as they stand up for their beliefs.

Much has been made of Generation Z's insistence on safety by other generations. But again, I reiterate the fact that this generation has only lived in a world of threats. Besides the large events mentioned in the opening of this chapter, let's also remember that this is a generation that has never gone to school without the very real possibility that they could die there in a mass shooting. Bullying also got a mighty ally in social media. Now there is literally nowhere to run from someone who decides to try to ruin your life by posting things online.

Collectively, our mental health has suffered, but again, Gen Z has carried that load from childhood. The epidemic of loneliness that U.S. Surgeon General Vivek Murthy has warned us about is certainly prevalent among Gen Z. In a study of eighth, tenth, and twelfth graders conducted annually from 1991 to 2021, measuring feelings of loneliness remained relatively stable in the 20-30 percent range until 2012, when they increased significantly. Of course, in the pandemic, these kids named loneliness and isolation as something they struggled with, but even in 2019, more than a third of them named that pain.[26] Across the board, Gen Z experiences a higher likelihood of dissatisfaction with life, depression, anxiety, and self-harm than other generations.[27]

Study after study credits social media as significant in deteriorating mental health. Certainly, social media results in weaponized bullying and creates unrealistic standards that kids cannot live up to, thanks to curated content and filters. Another factor, though, that is less quantifiable is simply that life has sucked for this generation since birth. We know we are in a season of apocalypse because real-life end-of-the-world scenarios are always accompanied by an uptick in apocalyptic literature

---

[26] Jean Twenge, *Generations*, 393.

[27] Jean Twenge, *Generations*, 394-400.

or artistic expression. This generation was raised on *The Hunger Games, The Walking Dead,* Hulu's *The Handmaid's Tale, Avengers: Infinity War,* and *Avengers: End Game,* just to name a few. Practically all of pop culture tells this generation stories of the world coming to an end because, on some level, that is what their whole life feels like. What other generations may see as fantastical tales, Gen Z sees as morality plays or as allegories for what they experience daily.

It is important to remember, however, that each of these stories ultimately reaches a point where good triumphs, and the world on the other side of the apocalypse is better. Despite no personal model that things can be otherwise, Gen Z is leading a fight to get to a better place. Whether it is the teenage activism of Malala Yousafzai and Greta Thunberg, or the prophetic action of young athletes like Naomi Osaka and Simone Biles stepping out of competition to engage in self-care, they are setting early examples for us of another way of being. They are fighting the prophetic battle through the apocalypse to lead us to a better place. We should acknowledge and support that and fight alongside them, rather than ridiculing them because they have to do it from their parents' basements. Those are the conditions we gave them. Let's not judge them for having to live in a world we built. Let's work with them to bring the light and life of the reign of God into this dark and difficult place.

Discussion Questions:

1. In what ways does Gen Z's apocalyptic worldview help them see injustice clearly—and how can older generations learn from that perspective?

2. How does Daniel's ability to resist the empire while remaining faithful speak to Gen Z's desire for authenticity and moral clarity?

3. What parallels do you see between the coded language in Daniel and the cultural slang and algorithm-driven realities of Gen Z?

4. How might churches and faith communities respond to Gen Z's critiques in ways that are humble, faithful, and constructive?

5. How does Daniel's story offer Gen Z—and all of us—a model for resilient, justice-oriented faith in the face of systemic pressure?

Gen X Prophets

The Satirists

Rather than pinning down to one person, it is a collective way of using voice that speaks into and for this generation. For a generation fluent in sarcasm, satirists have highlighted societal injustices with humor. In his work on *The Daily Show,* Jon Stewart captured the *zeitgeist* of a generation coming into its own, just as that generation confronted the reality of trying to find their place in a world where the Boomers switched from promising to change the world to starting to defend it, to the point of excluding Gen X from a place in that world. Stewart also nurtured talent, creating a line of prophetic disciples who continue this work, including Stephen Colbert and Trevor Noah. Matt Stone and Trey Parker, the creators of *South Park,* are prophets who speak for a generation from within their own generation (both are Gen X), creating the most popular show on television among Gen Xers during their college years and continuing to offer biting social satire as of the time of this publication. All the satirists have pointed out the hypocrisy of our social structures, including (even especially) critiquing religious hierarchies. Yet their goal is not simply to tear down, though some would accuse them of such. Their goal is a more just, more loving, more caring world. They are just using laughter to get us there.

CHAPTER SIX
Hosea and Gen X
(b. 1965-1980)

Don't You Forget About Me. Or Do. Whatever.

Silents. Boomers. Millennials. Gen Z. Wait. Aren't we forgetting one?

We wouldn't be alone. When CBS News did a story about the generations in early 2019, a graphic included the list of generations formatted like this:

- **The Silent Generation:** Born 1928-1945 (73-90 years old)
- **Baby Boomers:** Born 1946-1964 (54-72 years old)
- **Millennials:** Born 1981-1996 (22-37 years old)
- **Post-millennials:** Born 1997-present (0-21 years old)

Apparently, according to CBS, no one was born between 1965 and 1980. Can you imagine the panic that must have caused!? No wonder there was an energy crisis at the time. I am sure people were terrified as they imagined having to support the Boomers as they retired with only grandchildren who appeared from nowhere to support them!

It should be noted that the missing generation, Gen X, is known for its love of sarcasm. It should also be noted that I belong to Gen X.

My sarcasm at that omission was matched by many others of this nonexistent, forgotten generation. Read just a few of the responses to that news report that popped up on Twitter (now X, and appropriately owned by Xer Elon Musk):

> *"As a member of Gen X, I am 100% cool with being left out of this mess."*
>
> **Patton Oswalt**

> *"Er, you forgot one, CBSN Live. #GenX? You may remember us as the inventors of Harry Potter, podcasting, and irony."*
>
> **Rico Gagliano**

> *"You may know us as the ones currently shoring up boomer Social Security benefits, while probably not being able to retire ourselves."*
>
> **Larisa Breton**

Or, in perhaps the most Gen X response to being ignored and left out of time and space, Bill Evenson simply responded, "Glad that's settled."

This generation pairs well with another largely forgotten prophet: Hosea. Hosea, like Gen X, sits sandwiched between the major and minor prophets of the Bible. Technically, Hosea is a minor prophet. It is arguable, however, that neither the major nor the minor prophets would like to claim Hosea. But that is probably just fine with him. Hosea is sort of the anti-prophet of the prophetic books. Not ridiculous like Jonah, but instead biting and somewhat violent. Hosea participates in the work of prophets by engaging in prophetic actions. But who expects the prophetic action to be divorcing and remarrying a prostitute, sometimes leaving her children with the burden of illegitimacy and sometimes including them wholeheartedly in the family?

Like Gen X, Hosea really stands rebelliously outside the mold, begging us to forget it, but also at the same time, standing between the world of what was and what is to come and holding it all together. Hosea stands in the middle of the prophets—the first of the minor prophets, though it is longer than Daniel, who is still counted as a major prophet—just like Gen X stands in the middle of the generations right now and still gets forgotten like the ignored middle child. And like a true Gen Xer, we can see Hosea sitting sarcastically as the world crumbles around him, probably singing, "Clowns to the left of me, jokers to the right ... here I am, stuck in the middle with you."[28]

Fluent in Sarcasm

When I was in seminary, we had a weekly e-newsletter. At some point, they started asking people to share their favorite Bible verse. In what must have been a true mark that Gen X was alive and well on campus, one of my colleagues chose this verse: "Then the Lord said to me again, 'Go, make love to a woman who has a lover and is involved in adultery, just as the Lord loves the people of Israel, though they turn to other gods and love raisin cakes'" (Hosea 3:1).

---

[28] Stealers Wheel, "Stuck in the Middle with You," on *Stealers Wheel*, A&M Records, 1973, LP.

Got it: no religious adultery and no raisin cakes. Wait, what?!?!? This verse seems to equate the eating of raisin cakes with adultery or idolatry. What's up with the raisin cakes? Anyone else find that strangely disruptive to the prophetic word?

That is the work of sarcasm. Sarcasm is the art of saying something in an expected manner but with some small twist to it—either a tone of voice that just seems a little too flat or too excited for the moment, or a small turn of phrase that seems like it fits at first blush, but then you do sort of a mental double take that makes you wonder what the person is really saying. It might even prompt you to say, "Wait, are you being sarcastic?" A question which will often be greeted by an enthusiastic, "No!" or even a "Me?! Sarcastic?! I would never!"

There are several Gen X TikTokers out there who are masters of sarcasm, but one of my favorites is DadBod Veteran. He uses parody and sarcasm hand in hand as he leans off the railing of his porch, opining as one of the great elders, telling tales of old and imparting wisdom, all while he subtly (or not so subtly) engages in the major pastime of Gen X right now—ridiculing all the other generations around us.

Our ridicule is not truly that of animosity (well, most of the time). It is just the nature of being sandwiched between all the other generations right now. We understand the upbringing of the Silents and the Boomers, because we, too, rode bikes to our friends' houses and didn't grow up with cell phones. And we understand the tech reality of Millennials and Gen Z, because we exited college and entered the workforce just as the internet, email, and even cell phones (though certainly not smartphones) were becoming daily realities. Sometimes when I talk about the Gen X position in technology, I say, "Boomers may have invented the internet, and Millennials made it cool, but Gen X built it."

We truly are the generation smushed in between the most radical shift in human culture since either the Industrial Revolution or the Age of Exploration. That could make us a generation that bridges people and brings us together. However, because we are small and have been characterized as the generation everyone should skip, we instead become the people all too often who stand on the sidelines and, as Gen Xer Kenan Thompson once quipped in a *Saturday Night Live* skit, "Watch the world burn."[29]

Likewise, serving as God's prophet necessarily puts that person in an in-between position. Prophets are intermediaries between God and the people. We have seen how some prophets, like Jeremiah, are all in on experiencing the same fate as the people. Hosea ... not so much. Oh, his prophetic actions definitely reflect what happens to the people. But the actions he takes tend to have a greater impact on others than on himself—specifically, his family. While Gen X, in general, views the world with Hosea's biting sarcasm and takes his removed position, we also share in the experience of his children as the

---

[29] "Millennial Millions," *Saturday Night Live*, Season 47, Episode 8. Originally aired December 11, 2021, NBC.

generation that has been inflicted with the consequences of our elders' decisions.

Children of Divorce

One of the pastoral care concerns people continue to bring to me is worries about the stigma of divorce. Such stigma has all but disappeared everywhere EXCEPT the church. Too many of my people have been cast out or, at least, shamed out of other congregations or denominations because of divorce. It is profoundly heartbreaking to me that a situation that already comes with such heartache and trauma is compounded by the acts and judgment of so many Christians.

Hosea isn't helping things, either. Hosea uses divorce as a tool of shame—to shame a woman and to shame a nation. Hosea's chief prophetic act is to marry Gomer, a prostitute (probably a cultic prostitute working in another god's temple), and have three children with her. The action is meant to represent God accepting the people after they have started worshiping other gods. But then, as they attempt to do it again, Hosea divorces Gomer. As he does so, he also gives the children names representing that rejection—Not My People, No Mercy, and Jezreel.[30] And then Hosea remarries Gomer in

---

[30] Hosea does not ever change Jezreel's name, but it is likely that the people would have recognized a change in meaning of his name in the two contexts. The valley of Jezreel sits between mountains in the Holy Land. It is one of the flattest stretches of land in the entire area. In times of peace, the valley is incredibly green and fertile and provides sustenance for thousands of people. In times of war, however, it makes an ideal battlefield—plenty of room for thousands to fight and mountains for commanders to call the action. In times of war, it would be a field of blood and death. Thus, depending on whether the people are at peace or at war with God, Jezreel's name would have a different connotation.

an act of representing God's willingness to be in covenant with the people again. At the remarriage, Hosea gives the children new names—My People, Mercy, and Jezreel.

I have to wonder how those children felt. I only have to wonder, though, because I was one of the Gen X kids whose parents actually stayed married. Many of my friends had divorced parents and know exactly how it felt. Statistically, Gen Xers and Millennials have experienced higher divorce rates than Boomers and Silents[31] (Gen Z is just choosing not to get married, avoiding the whole complication altogether).[32] The difference is that when Boomers and Silents were getting divorced, the general societal stigma was still pretty strong. And while they were not the ones making the decisions to get divorced, Gen X kids carried the stigma of the decisions their parents (and even sometimes their grandparents) were making.[33] People whispered, "That child comes from a broken home." Kids truly wondered if there was anything they could have done to keep their parents together or if there was anything they could do to get their parents back together (thanks, *The Parent Trap)*.

Carrying the stigma for decisions we didn't make has contributed to Gen X's rejection of so much of society. That rebellion and rejection are the source of our generation's name, actually. Have you ever wondered why we suddenly

---

[31] Jean Twenge, *Generations*, 160.

[32] Jean Twenge, *Generations*, 375-378.

[33] Haydn Shaw, *Sticking Points*, 93.

started alphabetizing generations at X? It was never meant to be alphabetization! While others tried to brand us the slacker generation, we took matters into our own hands and demanded to be called Generation X—X because we didn't want to be labeled! We didn't want to be pigeonholed into someone else's ideas of us. We wanted our own identity, our own destiny, apart from the decisions and demands of the generations before us, or the ones that would come after us, for that matter.

But we were misunderstood and instead became a tool for labeling the generations that would come after us. Millennials were briefly called Gen Y. Gen Z is going to stick, and it looks like Gen Alpha will carry it on. It wasn't our choice, you generations after us. Ironically, Boomers and Silents took the name we had chosen to defy labels and made it into one. The very thing we fought not to be—a label—has become our defining identity. There is perhaps no more labeled generation alive today than X—the MTV Generation raised on brands and mass marketing like none have ever been or probably ever will be, as marketing becomes more and more niche with each passing day.

I feel like the children of Hosea feel us. Like all the people in Scripture, they "get" what we had to go through. They became the tools for social transformation that their dad wanted. Gen X, as a generation, also had to enact the social changes that the Boomers proclaimed. Boomers sought civil rights, women's rights, and gay rights. Gen X was the first generation of fully integrated classrooms, of women entering the workforce in significant numbers, and of trying to wrestle with LGBTQIA+ identity in the shadow of the AIDS crisis. And while all of these things have led to tremendous positive changes in our world, just remember that Gen X carries the scars on our backs from making it happen, much like Hosea's kids carried the responsibility of representing the relationship of God to the people. Even if those children tried to forge their own identity, Dad wouldn't let them. They are stuck in a prophetic word as representatives of the reality of others, just as Gen X represents the way things were and are simultaneously. And I can hear the resounding response from the children of Hosea to Generation X. A resounding …

"Whatever."

Promises, Promises

All that talk about marrying a woman and divorcing her and remarrying her—it makes Hosea ethically and theologically problematic. It is also confusing to study. On the plus side, however, it illustrates beautifully how frustrating it must be for Hosea to keep delivering the same word of God; the people get it for a while, only to revert to their old ways. Again, all the prophets confront this particularly irritating human trait, but perhaps because Hosea so personally bears this reality on the backs of his family, it feels just a bit more painful.

Likewise, Gen X is the generation carrying on our backs the pain of the societal transitions we have collectively gone through. We are the generation that saw pensions taken away from us before we were ready to make the shift to 401(k)s. We have had to shoulder the weight of the Boomers' retirement while we waited for enough Millennials and Gen Z to hit the workforce and cover Social Security. While much has been made about the fact that Millennials can't advance in their careers or buy houses because Boomers won't vacate positions or real estate fast enough, try being in the generation that is just going to give up and retire without ever getting a shot at that kind of advancement or ownership.

Haydn Shaw names one of Gen X's generational ghost stories as "Downward Mobility." Our parents lived the promises of the prosperous 1950s. Our kids enjoyed the optimistic childhoods of the 1990s. We got the energy crisis of the 1970s. As Shaw points out, "Gen X missed the growth of the economy but arrived just in time for the growth in prices"[34] (I feel like we need to fist bump our Gen Z comrades on that one). Despite having a reputation as slackers, many of us work what is referred to as an "extreme job," which demands more than sixty-hour work weeks, short deadlines, and 24/7 accessibility.[35]

Hosea and his family carried the weight of a nation as it went through some pretty terrible times. The prophet's family literally lived that national reality out in microcosm. The same can be said for Gen X. It really is not shocking,

---

[34] Haydn Shaw, *Sticking Points*, 97.

[35] Haydn Shaw, *Sticking Points*, 99.

then, that we are fluent in sarcasm. What is shocking is that we still have hope.

We're Never Going Out of Business

In a comedy sketch entitled "Every Generation Explained" on *Dry Bar Comedy,* stand-up comedian Karen Morgan describes Gen X as "the secret dive bar that only the locals know about. We don't have to advertise, and we're never going out of business." She then proceeds to take us through many of the things that Gen X survived. We were latchkey kids who raised ourselves. We sat in the way, way back of station wagons, rolling around with no seatbelts. Our parents blamed us for getting injured and told us to rub some dirt on our injuries and to quit crying. We ate out of lunchboxes filled with rust. We survived rubber dodge balls in gym class. We got shoved outside to play with the door locked behind us, living on hose water. We had rock fights and BB gun fights. We made homemade bike ramps and rode with no bike helmets.[36]

While she is a comedian and deliberately overemphasizes the feral childhoods of Gen Xers, she also isn't wrong. Being the squished generation between a generation who had mothers who were not in the workforce (Boomers) in significant numbers and a generation raised by helicopter parents (Millennials), we were the wild kids out there

---

[36] Karen Morgan, "Every Generation Explained," *Dry Bar Comedy,* posted May 14, 2023, on YouTube, https://www.youtube.com/watch?v=Edxr25t8trc&list=PLxB23mVwj7uxTElEAe5dFjEmbhOuOy0SY&index=3.

raising ourselves, a bit like the *Lord of the Flies.* It raised a pretty tough generation, a generation that other generations are warned on TikTok not to wake up because we actually know how to fight. We are the generation that invented grunge, a musical expression of our rough and cynical ways.

We are also a generation, though, that won't give up. We are tough. And we see ourselves like cockroaches, the most likely generation to survive a world-ending event like a nuclear holocaust. Whether that is true or not really doesn't matter. We hang our hats on such tenacious resilience. No matter what, we will persevere. We are, in fact, never going out of business.

That is the hope of all the prophets. That no matter what, God's people will persevere. Hosea is no exception. And Hosea is a good companion for Gen X, because Hosea saw some things. Hosea lived some things. Hosea said some things. And Hosea is still part of God's story to this very day. Not quite a major prophet but not really minor either, Hosea stands in the middle and gets ignored quite a bit, but perseveres anyway. The prophetic witness of Gen X and Hosea is that no matter what life throws at us and no matter how pushed to the side we may feel, we are still here, and we are still part of God's witness of resurrection to the world.

And we're never going out of business.

Discussion Questions:

1. How does Hosea's use of symbolic relationships reflect Gen X's experience of being shaped by others' choices and traumas?

2. What does Gen X's reputation for sarcasm reveal about its coping mechanisms and role as a cultural "middle child"?

3. In what ways does Hosea's story of naming and renaming mirror Gen X's struggle with identity and labeling across generations?

4. How do economic shifts like the loss of pensions or the rise of gig work shape the spiritual and prophetic voice of Gen X?

5. What lessons can the church and society learn from the persistence and overlooked witness of Hosea—and of Generation X?

CHAPTER SEVEN
...The Generations

A noticeable pattern emerged as we made our way through these generations as a church. We alternate back and forth between a generation that pushes the prophetic envelope, taking a bold stance to move society into a new way of being, and a generation that has to deal with the repercussions of the movements of the previous one.

While we did not discuss them much in this book, the Greatest Generation took a stand against fascism on a global scale, but did so definitively through the use of potentially world-ending nuclear power. The Silent Generation had to get everyone to settle down and play nice as a result of that power being unleashed in the world. The Baby Boomers significantly advanced our society through the great social movements of civil rights, women's rights, LGBTQIA+ rights, and disability rights. Gen X had to live that reality out on the ground as the first generation to spend our whole educational career in integrated classrooms, as a generation raised by two working parents without childcare infrastructure in place to support that reality, as a generation who collectively feared AIDS more than any other generation while working out what acceptance meant in the midst of that threat, and as a generation too small to support the cost of changing infrastructure to allow greater accessibility. The Millennials have pushed us forward in social change and collective empowerment through movements like the Arab Spring that were enabled by social media, and Gen Z will have to figure out what it means to be human in light of AI and how to create a more civil society in a world ruled by internet trolls.

We could call this alternating pattern the idealist-realist seesaw. It can also be described for our purposes as the prophetic-pastoral tension. This pattern may be why we feel like we have more in common with our grandparents than our parents. It is also why it feels increasingly difficult to respect one another. Idealist generations feel that the generation that followed them has reverted back instead of carrying their mission forward. Realist generations feel like the generation that preceded them has no idea how hard it is to actually live with the "mess" the previous generation created.

These generational echoes can bond us—or divide us, depending on how we handle the tension. The vitriol among the generations only serves to further divide us. Millennials no longer return home for Thanksgiving, choosing Friendsgiving instead, because they simply can't handle the ways their parents and grandparents talk around the table. Gen Z knows they aren't living up to the idealism of their parents, and so they are becoming the most isolated generation our world has ever produced. We are so deeply and collectively rooted in our own generational perspectives that we fail to notice how we are all part of the same unfolding narrative, and we all have a responsibility for where we are all placed within that narrative. If we saw our connections instead of our divisions, maybe we would treat one another with greater kindness and generosity and look more hopefully at our collective future.

It is very difficult to look past our historical moment, though. We see that truth in the prophets. They became prophets not because times were smooth sailing and easygoing. They are prophets either because a storm is looming or a storm is upon them, usually in the form of an invading army. The pressure of history is very literally crushing in upon them. In moments like that, it is very difficult to see a future. Yet that is also what the prophets did: they laid claim to the future, particularly the future God had in store for them. "I know the plans I have in mind for you, declares the Lord; they are plans for peace, not disaster, to give you a future filled with hope" (Jer 29:11).

The prophets stand on the assumption that, no matter what the present looks like, God's got this. The current reality is not the ultimate reality! But just like the push and pull among the generations, the prophets acknowledge that living through to get to that reality involves both hope and lamentation, victory and loss, life and death all at once. Living into the plans that God has for us is not easy. Some generations will pay the price for the decisions made by the generations before them. They always do. But the prophets stand on the hope that our own 20th-century prophet

Martin Luther King Jr. said (that was a paraphrase of a sermon from abolitionist pastor Theodore Parker), "The arc of the moral universe is long, but it bends toward justice."[37]

The lived reality of our current generations and the idealistic promise of the prophets meet in one location, and one location only, in our world today: the church. There is no other collective entity left in our society where all eight currently alive generations regularly interact with one another than the church. That's right, I said eight. I still have people in my congregation who were born before 1925— the Greatest Generation—and 2025 marks the year that Generation Beta is born.[38] As the last remaining collective social and cultural gathering point in the history of all living humans, the church has profound significance and relevance for our world. We can be the meeting point and understanding point of the generations that will help us learn to love and live with one another better. As such, we can serve as the prophetic sign to the world of the transcendent power of God's love, affirming the continuous unfolding of God's and humanity's story.

To do this, though, we have to behave better. Currently, the church often acts like the world. We are dividing up, one way or another. The most damaging way we divide up

---

[37] For a discussion of the origins of this quote, which also shows how generation after generation has to stand on and reinterpret the past to keep moving forward, see Mychal Denzel Smith, "The Truth About 'The Arc of the Moral Universe,'" *HuffPost*, January 18, 2018, https://www.huffpost.com/entry/opinion-smith-obama-king_n_5a5903e0e4b04f3c55a252a4.

[38] For an example of the discussion on the arrival of Generation Beta, see Esther Sun, "From Boomers to Gen Beta: A Guide to the Generation Names," *Today Online*, January 9, 2025, https://www.today.com/parents/teens/generation-names-rcna137457.

is when one generation insists that their perspective is the only valued one or is the one that should be in charge. Those days are long gone. We now live in a society where even young children grow up with a sense of agency, voice, and participation—in families, classrooms, and online platforms alike. The church needs to reflect that collective and cross-generational empowerment, not because that is how the world works now, but because that is how God hoped we would always be. Isaiah reminds us that in a world of peace, "a little child will lead" us (Isa 11:6). And yes, that is an oracle about the Messiah, but it is also a proclamation of what God's reign looks like. Seems to me like we could use a lot more of what God's reign looks like in our world today, so let's empower all the generations to be part of that effort instead of insisting one is in charge.

Another way the church divides is by focusing too much on stage-of-life ministries. We send people to groups solely based on their age. Now, don't get me wrong; there can be something very helpful about being with people our own age. It is especially helpful for people growing in their faith and lives to ensure they receive appropriate instruction tailored to their age (in other words, keep children and youth ministries separate, of course). I am not advocating for the elimination of stage-of-life ministries altogether. I am saying, however, that we should be intentional in creating spaces where those age divides are eliminated.

I mentioned at the beginning that this book evolved from a sermon series we conducted in 2023. There was a little more to it than just a run-of-the-mill series. It was summer, after all, so we had a little fun. Everyone was encouraged to dress in the style of the era we were celebrating that week. Each worship service included songs reflective of the era. The opening welcome was filled with slang of the featured period, and we highlighted important events that were happening at the time (I chose a specific year for each welcome). We also talked about what life in our town was like (including noting population totals and how many stoplights or stop signs were in town that year). At the end of the series, we celebrated that all of us are part of God's family and that all our histories have a place in God's story. I called out each generation and invited them to stand. We looked around at all of the room and cheered that we are all beloved people of God.

That afternoon, we capped off the celebration with an intergenerational dance. We played music from the 1950s to the 2020s. All the generations were there, and each generation took the spotlight, teaching the other generations their dances. The clear winner of the day was "The Cha Cha Slide," which my Millennial best friend had told me was necessary to include. Apparently, it shows up at every wedding these days, and enough generations have been to enough weddings that nearly all of us know it. The surprise of the day was "The Cotton-Eyed Joe," which is a late Gen X/ early Millennial song, but Gen Alpha was best at teaching it to us. They all learn it at summer camp!

I have never been in a room with such collective joy in all my life. That series, and that dance, marked a significant shift in our church community. Suddenly, we could name how much we all want to be together. Intergenerational interaction has become an intentional focus of our work together. We now have adult Sunday school classes that are advertised as open to all generations. This year, in place of the dance, we are trying an intergenerational talent show. The rules are simple: no solo acts allowed, and every act must contain people from at least two different generations. Also, this summer we are trying an experiment called 4S: Second Saturday Supper and Stories. On the second Saturday of each month, we will gather around a theme in our fellowship hall, share food together, and share stories related to each theme. We start with "Family Vacations."

As a pastor, my other challenge is making sure to speak into the perspectives of all these generations. The result sometimes looks rather scattered and chaotic. It means one Sunday I may be preaching against the dangers of the highly militarized perspective of Christian Nationalism, and then the next Sunday, reminding us to pray for and honor our fallen soldiers on Memorial Day. Those sermons are not actually in opposition to one another, but trust me when I say they feel very different to my Silent Generation and my Gen Z young adults. Because we are intentional about creating space for intergenerational interaction, though, for the most part, we collectively understand that all of us will feel at home sometimes and feel uncomfortably challenged sometimes.

Which brings us back to the prophets. The prophets are

in the business of making us feel uncomfortable. They are doing so because we are not yet living in the reign of God, and the prophets, more than anything, want to bring us there. Moving from the divisiveness and vitriol of this world (then and now) to the love and fullness of God's reign is a painful experience. It is beautiful when we get glimpses of that reign, though. And we know it is a place where we are all welcome—all generations through all of time who have sought the love of God and been sought by God.

So the last thing to recognize about the prophets, the ones we have studied here who are both timeless and time-bound, is that they, too, are part of the people and part of the times in which they were born, and they do not abandon God's people in the moment. Whatever happens to the people happens to them, too. They love the people enough to stay with them as history unfolds before them. May we remember that, too. May we love the people around us enough to enter gratefully into the moments we get to share with them, even if the view we have from our perspectives looks different. And may we seek to understand the views of the ones around us, as they might understand ours as well. And when we do, when we see each other more clearly because we have sought that understanding, may we love one another better. And may we dance together in the welcoming grace of the God who loves us all, no matter what generation.

Discussion Questions:

1. The chapter describes a pattern of alternating "prophetic" and "pastoral" (or "idealist" and "realist") generations. Which generation do you identify with most, and do you see yourself as more prophetic or pastoral in your outlook? How do you see this pattern playing out in your own family or community?

2. The author argues that the church is "the last remaining collective social and cultural gathering point" for all generations. Do you agree? What are some practical ways your church—or another community—could foster more meaningful intergenerational interaction?

3. How can churches strike a balance between honoring the perspectives of older generations and empowering younger ones, especially when they may disagree on core social or theological issues?

4. Reflect on the author's statement: "Current reality is not ultimate reality!" How does this align with the prophetic imagination in Scripture? What are the challenges of holding on to hope when cultural or church conflict feels overwhelming?

5. The chapter ends with a celebration of joy and connection through a multi-generational dance. What are modern "dances" your community could create—literal or metaphorical—that help different generations move together in love and grace?